THIS JOURNAL BELONGS TO

Introduction

A few years ago, I had an epiphany: I'd done countless things that made my life happier, and yet too often, I felt stuck in my head—disconnected from the world and other people, and also from myself. After an eye-opening trip to the doctor, I realized: I needed to connect with my five senses.

While researching my book *Life in Five Senses*, I discovered that, by tuning in to my senses, I could transform my everyday life by paying attention to the richness of the physical world around me.

Now more than ever, it's easy to get stuck in our heads or behind a screen, and forget to engage with the world around us. It's also easy to fall into ruts of experience. Tapping in to our senses can awaken our mindfulness and revive our sense of excitement, connection, gratitude, and wonder.

Each of us engages with the world through our own particular complement of senses, whatever those might be. This journal is designed to help you explore your own sensory world, and discover how you might use your senses to cheer up, calm down, live in the moment, find more pleasure and more energy, deepen your connections, spark your creativity, and even touch the transcendent.

Onward,
GRETCHEN RUBIN

How to use this journal

Every day, check in with each of your five senses and record your observations. What did you see, hear, smell, taste, touch? You might write down your favorite sensations from the day, create a daily practice of checking in at certain times, or seek out sensory experiences and note their effect.

Each month, pay special attention to one of your senses.

MONTH	DAY	YEAR
April	1	2024

See	I kept looking at the granola bar wrapper on my desk. Once I finally threw it away I was much less distracted. Lesson learned, take the time to keep my desk cleared off.
Hear	Walking downtown, heard church bells chime the hour
Smell	Barnaby needs a bath
Taste	Surprising, delicious smoky flavor in a salad
Touch	Scratchy sisal rug at my in-laws' apartment

For five months, you'll also be prompted to pay special attention to one sense in particular, with extra entry space for that sense. And for the sixth month, you'll be prompted to pay special attention to how your senses work together.

Start any time, and go in any order you want.

MONTH April	DAY 2	YEAR 2024

See	Gorgeous silvery black fur of a Weimaraner dog, looked frosted
Hear	A/C humming
Smell	Delicious cooking smells coming from the neighbor's house
Taste	The unusual spice flavors used in a patty at lunch
Touch	Dry skin - need to keep lotion at my desk

For the final month of entries, pay attention to how your senses work together. Record observations from experiences that combine multiple senses. Note any memories that may arise.

You might record meals with a sweetheart, playtime with your kids or a pet, doing a five-senses check-in at the end of your workday.

MONTH	DAY	YEAR
October	2	2024

Observation

I had an apple for a snack today—I noticed the patterns in the red and yellow-green skin, and the weight meant it was going to be juicy. It made a satisfying crunch when I bit into it, and it tasted sweet and a little tangy.

SENSES USED
Check all that apply.

See ☑ Hear ☑ Smell ☑ Taste ☑ Touch ☑

MONTH	DAY	YEAR
October	3	2024

Observation

I took the Five-Senses Quiz and my most neglected sense is taste, so I went to a wine shop downtown and did a tasting. I like wine with dinner but usually don't pay much attention to it. Tasting several wines side by side really highlighted the different flavors and now the tasting notes make a lot more sense.

SENSES USED
Check all that apply.

See ☑ Hear ☐ Smell ☑ Taste ☑ Touch ☐

Record observations from each sense, or the overall effect.

MONTH	DAY	YEAR
October	4	2024

Observation

Didn't sleep well last night and really felt it today. My body felt sluggish and my eyes were tired. Ambient noises like the A/C humming seemed extra loud. A quick afternoon walk to get a cup of coffee perked me up.

SENSES USED
Check all that apply.

See Hear Smell Taste Touch

Seek out experiences that stimulate multiple senses.

MONTH	DAY	YEAR

Observation

SENSES USED
Check all that apply.

See Hear Smell Taste Touch

At the end of each month, you have the opportunity to create a five-senses portrait of any subject you choose.

You might create portraits of people, places, or experiences in your life right now, or dive into your memories to capture portraits from the past. You might choose a different subject each month, or choose the same subject to record how your perception changes over time.

Observe a person, place, or experience more vividly by capturing the sensations you associate with it.

Monthly Five-Senses Portrait

Pick a subject for this month's five-senses portrait. You can choose a person, a pet, a place, a trip, a city, yourself, or any other subject you can think of. Identify the sights, sounds, smells, tastes, and touch of all the things and experiences you associate with the subject you chose.

DATE 05 | 31 | 24

WHEN I THINK OF...
Write the subject of this month's five-senses portrait.

Aaron

I THINK OF SEEING...

- The way he folds back newspapers as he reads them
- Our coat closet full of his jackets
- Him stretched out on the sofa for a Sunday nap
- The striking colors of the rose-red fleece jacket he often wears
-

I THINK OF HEARING...

- His voice saying, "Let's gaze lovingly" before cracking open the
- door so we could peek at Eliza, then Eleanor, asleep in a crib
- Sports talk on his favorite podcast
- His voice discussing business jargon I don't understand
- His long, slow breaths when he is in a very deep sleep

I THINK OF SMELLING...

- His botanical scented soap
- His morning coffee brewing
- The hot dog cart in the park he loves to smell (but never buys one)
-
-

I THINK OF TASTING...

- The coffee he just drank when I kiss him goodbye
- Curry from our favorite take-out spot
- Rum and Cokes he drank when we met in college
-
-

I THINK OF TOUCHING...

- His scratchy stubble when he needs to shave
- His heavy winter sweaters
- His cold feet when he gets in bed
- Warm, long hugs
-

When you reach the end of this journal, reflect on your experiences over the last six months. How did your awareness of each sense change? How do you feel now compared to when you started this journal?

Sensory Highlights

Reflect on the last six months.

You might use different colors to fill in ratings when you begin this journal and when you finish.

EVALUATE YOUR SENSES

On a scale of 1 to 10, rate how aware you are of each of your five senses.
1=need to work more on this sense, 10=mastered this sense entirely

SEEING

HEARING

SMELLING

TASTING

TOUCHING

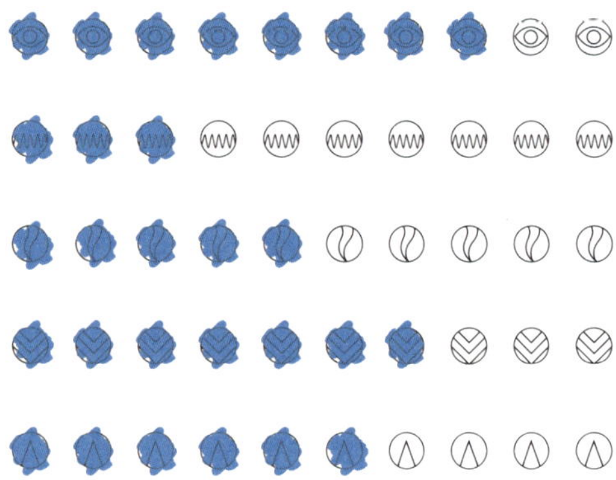

Consider how you might apply the self-knowledge you've gained from this exploration.

REFLECTIONS

Record your thoughts, highlights, and what you've learned.

It's easiest for me to recall visual information, and most of my memories are visual. Once I started paying attention, I realized that sounds caused the most distractions or negative experiences. Look into white noise machine, noise-cancelling headphones.

These pages offer different ways to think about your experience—you can evaluate each sense, take notes about what you've learned, and create timelines to record the highlights of your explorations.

"SEEING" HIGHLIGHTS OF YOUR SIX MONTHS

Add dates and memories related to your sense of seeing. Fill in as little or as much as you want.

Recording sensory information can help keep memories vivid.

05 / 16 / 24 → Caught a glimpse of a comet right before dawn when we went camping

06 / 03 / 24 → Loved watching the waves crash on the cliffs at our local beach.

06 / 20 / 24 → Longest day of the year, beautiful sunset

07 / 05 / 24 → Botanical garden - so many different colors of roses!

08 / 30 / 24 → Sun rays coming through storm clouds

09 / 22 / 24 → Eliza's dance recital was so fun to watch

/ / →

/ / →

/ / →

/ / →

MONTH ONE

This month pay special attention to your sense of

Seeing

"It's we who make the masterpiece."

–GRETCHEN RUBIN

MONTH	DAY	YEAR

See	
Hear	
Smell	
Taste	
Touch	

MONTH	DAY	YEAR

See	
Hear	
Smell	
Taste	
Touch	

MONTH	DAY	YEAR

See

Hear

Smell

Taste

Touch

MONTH	DAY	YEAR

See	
Hear	
Smell	
Taste	
Touch	

MONTH	DAY	YEAR

See	
Hear	
Smell	
Taste	
Touch	

MONTH	DAY	YEAR

See	
Hear	
Smell	
Taste	
Touch	

MONTH	DAY	YEAR

See	
Hear	
Smell	
Taste	
Touch	

MONTH	DAY	YEAR

See	
Hear	
Smell	
Taste	
Touch	

MONTH	DAY	YEAR

See	
Hear	
Smell	
Taste	
Touch	

MONTH	DAY	YEAR

See	
Hear	
Smell	
Taste	
Touch	

MONTH	DAY	YEAR

See	
Hear	
Smell	
Taste	
Touch	

MONTH	DAY	YEAR

See	
Hear	
Smell	
Taste	
Touch	

MONTH	DAY	YEAR

See	
Hear	
Smell	
Taste	
Touch	

MONTH	DAY	YEAR

See	
Hear	
Smell	
Taste	
Touch	

MONTH	DAY	YEAR

See	
Hear	
Smell	
Taste	
Touch	

MONTH	DAY	YEAR

See	
Hear	
Smell	
Taste	
Touch	

MONTH	DAY	YEAR

See

Hear

Smell

Taste

Touch

MONTH	DAY	YEAR

See	
Hear	
Smell	
Taste	
Touch	

MONTH	DAY	YEAR

See	
Hear	
Smell	
Taste	
Touch	

MONTH	DAY	YEAR

See	
Hear	
Smell	
Taste	
Touch	

MONTH	DAY	YEAR

See	
Hear	
Smell	
Taste	
Touch	

MONTH	DAY	YEAR

See	
Hear	
Smell	
Taste	
Touch	

MONTH	DAY	YEAR

See

Hear

Smell

Taste

Touch

MONTH	DAY	YEAR

See	
Hear	
Smell	
Taste	
Touch	

MONTH | DAY | YEAR

See	
Hear	
Smell	
Taste	
Touch	

MONTH	DAY	YEAR

See	
Hear	
Smell	
Taste	
Touch	

MONTH	DAY	YEAR

See	
Hear	
Smell	
Taste	
Touch	

MONTH	DAY	YEAR

See	
Hear	
Smell	
Taste	
Touch	

MONTH	DAY	YEAR

See	
Hear	
Smell	
Taste	
Touch	

MONTH	DAY	YEAR

See

Hear

Smell

Taste

Touch

MONTH	DAY	YEAR

See	
Hear	
Smell	
Taste	
Touch	

Monthly Five-Senses Portrait

Pick a subject for this month's five-senses portrait. You can choose a person, a pet, a place, a trip, a city, yourself, or any other subject you can think of. Identify the sights, sounds, smells, tastes, and touch of all the things and experiences you associate with the subject you chose.

DATE

WHEN I THINK OF...
Write the subject of this month's five-senses portrait.

I THINK OF SEEING...

-
-
-
-
-

I THINK OF HEARING...

-
-
-
-
-

I THINK OF SMELLING...

- ......
- ......
- ......
- ......
- ......

I THINK OF TASTING...

- ......
- ......
- ......
- ......
- ......

I THINK OF TOUCHING...

- ......
- ......
- ......
- ......
- ......

MONTH TWO

This month pay special attention to your sense of

Hearing

"Even disagreeable sensations can deepen experience."

–GRETCHEN RUBIN

MONTH	DAY	YEAR

Hear	
See	
Smell	
Taste	
Touch	

MONTH	DAY	YEAR

Hear	
See	
Smell	
Taste	
Touch	

MONTH	DAY	YEAR

Hear	
See	
Smell	
Taste	
Touch	

MONTH	DAY	YEAR

Hear	
See	
Smell	
Taste	
Touch	

MONTH	DAY	YEAR

Hear	
See	
Smell	
Taste	
Touch	

MONTH	DAY	YEAR

Hear	
See	
Smell	
Taste	
Touch	

MONTH	DAY	YEAR

Hear	
See	
Smell	
Taste	
Touch	

MONTH	DAY	YEAR

Hear

See

Smell

Taste

Touch

MONTH	DAY	YEAR

Hear

See

Smell

Taste

Touch

MONTH	DAY	YEAR

Hear	
See	
Smell	
Taste	
Touch	

MONTH	DAY	YEAR

Hear	
See	
Smell	
Taste	
Touch	

MONTH	DAY	YEAR

Hear	
See	
Smell	
Taste	
Touch	

MONTH	DAY	YEAR

Hear	
See	
Smell	
Taste	
Touch	

MONTH	DAY	YEAR

Hear	
See	
Smell	
Taste	
Touch	

MONTH	DAY	YEAR

Hear	
See	
Smell	
Taste	
Touch	

MONTH	DAY	YEAR

Hear	
See	
Smell	
Taste	
Touch	

MONTH	DAY	YEAR

Hear	
See	
Smell	
Taste	
Touch	

MONTH	DAY	YEAR

Hear	
See	
Smell	
Taste	
Touch	

MONTH	DAY	YEAR

Hear	
See	
Smell	
Taste	
Touch	

MONTH	DAY	YEAR

Hear	
See	
Smell	
Taste	
Touch	

MONTH	DAY	YEAR

Hear	
See	
Smell	
Taste	
Touch	

MONTH	DAY	YEAR

Hear	
See	
Smell	
Taste	
Touch	

MONTH	DAY	YEAR

Hear	
See	
Smell	
Taste	
Touch	

MONTH	DAY	YEAR

Hear	
See	
Smell	
Taste	
Touch	

MONTH	DAY	YEAR

Hear	
See	
Smell	
Taste	
Touch	

MONTH	DAY	YEAR

Hear	
See	
Smell	
Taste	
Touch	

MONTH	DAY	YEAR

Hear	
See	
Smell	
Taste	
Touch	

MONTH	DAY	YEAR

Hear	
See	
Smell	
Taste	
Touch	

MONTH	DAY	YEAR

Hear	
See	
Smell	
Taste	
Touch	

MONTH	DAY	YEAR

Hear	
See	
Smell	
Taste	
Touch	

MONTH	DAY	YEAR

Hear	
See	
Smell	
Taste	
Touch	

Monthly Five-Senses Portrait

Pick a subject for this month's five-senses portrait. You can choose a person, a pet, a place, a trip, a city, yourself, or any other subject you can think of. Identify the sights, sounds, smells, tastes, and touch of all the things and experiences you associate with the subject you chose.

DATE

WHEN I THINK OF...
Write the subject of this month's five-senses portrait.

I THINK OF SEEING...

-
-
-
-
-

I THINK OF HEARING...

-
-
-
-
-

I THINK OF SMELLING…

- ....
- ....
- ....
- ....
- ....

I THINK OF TASTING…

- ....
- ....
- ....
- ....
- ....

I THINK OF TOUCHING…

- ....
- ....
- ....
- ....
- ....

MONTH THREE

This month pay special attention to your sense of

Smelling

"We can't glut ourselves on perfume."

–GRETCHEN RUBIN

MONTH	DAY	YEAR

Smell	
See	
Hear	
Taste	
Touch	

MONTH	DAY	YEAR

Smell	
See	
Hear	
Taste	
Touch	

MONTH	DAY	YEAR

Smell	
See	
Hear	
Taste	
Touch	

MONTH	DAY	YEAR

Smell	
See	
Hear	
Taste	
Touch	

MONTH	DAY	YEAR

Smell	
See	
Hear	
Taste	
Touch	

MONTH	DAY	YEAR

Smell	
See	
Hear	
Taste	
Touch	

MONTH	DAY	YEAR

Smell	
See	
Hear	
Taste	
Touch	

MONTH	DAY	YEAR

Smell	
See	
Hear	
Taste	
Touch	

MONTH	DAY	YEAR

Smell	
See	
Hear	
Taste	
Touch	

MONTH	DAY	YEAR

Smell	
See	
Hear	
Taste	
Touch	

MONTH	DAY	YEAR

Smell	
See	
Hear	
Taste	
Touch	

MONTH	DAY	YEAR

Smell	
See	
Hear	
Taste	
Touch	

MONTH	DAY	YEAR

Smell

See

Hear

Taste

Touch

MONTH	DAY	YEAR

Smell	
See	
Hear	
Taste	
Touch	

MONTH	DAY	YEAR

Smell	
See	
Hear	
Taste	
Touch	

MONTH	DAY	YEAR

Smell	
See	
Hear	
Taste	
Touch	

MONTH	DAY	YEAR

Smell

See

Hear

Taste

Touch

MONTH	DAY	YEAR

Smell	
See	
Hear	
Taste	
Touch	

MONTH	DAY	YEAR

Smell	
See	
Hear	
Taste	
Touch	

MONTH	DAY	YEAR

Smell	
See	
Hear	
Taste	
Touch	

MONTH	DAY	YEAR

Smell	
See	
Hear	
Taste	
Touch	

MONTH	DAY	YEAR

Smell	
See	
Hear	
Taste	
Touch	

MONTH	DAY	YEAR

Smell	
See	
Hear	
Taste	
Touch	

MONTH	DAY	YEAR

Smell	
See	
Hear	
Taste	
Touch	

MONTH	DAY	YEAR

Smell	
See	
Hear	
Taste	
Touch	

MONTH | DAY | YEAR

Smell	
See	
Hear	
Taste	
Touch	

MONTH	DAY	YEAR

Smell	
See	
Hear	
Taste	
Touch	

MONTH | DAY | YEAR

Smell

See

Hear

Taste

Touch

MONTH	DAY	YEAR

Smell	
See	
Hear	
Taste	
Touch	

MONTH	DAY	YEAR

Smell	
See	
Hear	
Taste	
Touch	

MONTH	DAY	YEAR

Smell	
See	
Hear	
Taste	
Touch	

Monthly Five-Senses Portrait

Pick a subject for this month's five-senses portrait. You can choose a person, a pet, a place, a trip, a city, yourself, or any other subject you can think of. Identify the sights, sounds, smells, tastes, and touch of all the things and experiences you associate with the subject you chose.

DATE

WHEN I THINK OF...
Write the subject of this month's five-senses portrait.

I THINK OF SEEING...

-
-
-
-
-

I THINK OF HEARING...

-
-
-
-
-

I THINK OF SMELLING...

- ...
- ...
- ...
- ...
- ...

I THINK OF TASTING...

- ...
- ...
- ...
- ...
- ...

I THINK OF TOUCHING...

- ...
- ...
- ...
- ...
- ...

MONTH FOUR

This month pay special attention to your sense of

Tasting

"To recall a pleasure is to experience it twice."

–GRETCHEN RUBIN

MONTH	DAY	YEAR

Taste	
See	
Hear	
Smell	
Touch	

MONTH	DAY	YEAR

Taste	
See	
Hear	
Smell	
Touch	

MONTH	DAY	YEAR

Taste

See

Hear

Smell

Touch

MONTH	DAY	YEAR

Taste	
See	
Hear	
Smell	
Touch	

MONTH	DAY	YEAR

Taste	
See	
Hear	
Smell	
Touch	

MONTH	DAY	YEAR

Taste	
See	
Hear	
Smell	
Touch	

MONTH	DAY	YEAR

Taste	
See	
Hear	
Smell	
Touch	

MONTH	DAY	YEAR

Taste	
See	
Hear	
Smell	
Touch	

MONTH	DAY	YEAR

Taste	
See	
Hear	
Smell	
Touch	

MONTH	DAY	YEAR

Taste	
See	
Hear	
Smell	
Touch	

MONTH	DAY	YEAR

Taste	
See	
Hear	
Smell	
Touch	

MONTH	DAY	YEAR

Taste

See

Hear

Smell

Touch

MONTH	DAY	YEAR

Taste	
See	
Hear	
Smell	
Touch	

MONTH	DAY	YEAR

Taste	
See	
Hear	
Smell	
Touch	

MONTH	DAY	YEAR

Taste	
See	
Hear	
Smell	
Touch	

MONTH	DAY	YEAR

Taste	
See	
Hear	
Smell	
Touch	

MONTH	DAY	YEAR

Taste	
See	
Hear	
Smell	
Touch	

MONTH	DAY	YEAR

Taste	
See	
Hear	
Smell	
Touch	

MONTH	DAY	YEAR

Taste	
See	
Hear	
Smell	
Touch	

MONTH	DAY	YEAR

Taste	
See	
Hear	
Smell	
Touch	

MONTH	DAY	YEAR

Taste	
See	
Hear	
Smell	
Touch	

MONTH	DAY	YEAR

Taste	
See	
Hear	
Smell	
Touch	

MONTH	DAY	YEAR

Taste	
See	
Hear	
Smell	
Touch	

MONTH	DAY	YEAR

Taste	
See	
Hear	
Smell	
Touch	

MONTH	DAY	YEAR

Taste	
See	
Hear	
Smell	
Touch	

MONTH	DAY	YEAR

Taste	
See	
Hear	
Smell	
Touch	

MONTH | DAY | YEAR

Taste

See

Hear

Smell

Touch

MONTH	DAY	YEAR

Taste	
See	
Hear	
Smell	
Touch	

MONTH	DAY	YEAR

Taste	
See	
Hear	
Smell	
Touch	

MONTH	DAY	YEAR

Taste	
See	
Hear	
Smell	
Touch	

MONTH	DAY	YEAR

Taste	
See	
Hear	
Smell	
Touch	

Monthly Five-Senses Portrait

Pick a subject for this month's five-senses portrait. You can choose a person, a pet, a place, a trip, a city, yourself, or any other subject you can think of. Identify the sights, sounds, smells, tastes, and touch of all the things and experiences you associate with the subject you chose.

DATE

WHEN I THINK OF...
Write the subject of this month's five-senses portrait.

I THINK OF SEEING...

-
-
-
-
-

I THINK OF HEARING...

-
-
-
-
-

I THINK OF SMELLING...

- ....
- ....
- ....
- ....
- ....

I THINK OF TASTING...

- ....
- ....
- ....
- ....
- ....

I THINK OF TOUCHING...

- ....
- ....
- ....
- ....
- ....

MONTH FIVE

This month pay special attention to your sense of

Touching

"There's a big difference between a zoo and a petting zoo."

–GRETCHEN RUBIN

MONTH	DAY	YEAR

Touch	
See	
Hear	
Smell	
Taste	

MONTH	DAY	YEAR

Touch	
See	
Hear	
Smell	
Taste	

MONTH	DAY	YEAR

Touch	
See	
Hear	
Smell	
Taste	

MONTH	DAY	YEAR

Touch	
See	
Hear	
Smell	
Taste	

MONTH	DAY	YEAR

Touch	
See	
Hear	
Smell	
Taste	

MONTH	DAY	YEAR

Touch	
See	
Hear	
Smell	
Taste	

MONTH	DAY	YEAR

Touch

See

Hear

Smell

Taste

MONTH	DAY	YEAR

Touch	
See	
Hear	
Smell	
Taste	

MONTH	DAY	YEAR

Touch	
See	
Hear	
Smell	
Taste	

MONTH	DAY	YEAR

Touch	
See	
Hear	
Smell	
Taste	

MONTH	DAY	YEAR

Touch	
See	
Hear	
Smell	
Taste	

MONTH	DAY	YEAR

Touch	
See	
Hear	
Smell	
Taste	

MONTH	DAY	YEAR

Touch	
See	
Hear	
Smell	
Taste	

MONTH	DAY	YEAR

Touch	
See	
Hear	
Smell	
Taste	

MONTH	DAY	YEAR

Touch	
See	
Hear	
Smell	
Taste	

MONTH	DAY	YEAR

Touch	
See	
Hear	
Smell	
Taste	

MONTH	DAY	YEAR

Touch	
See	
Hear	
Smell	
Taste	

MONTH	DAY	YEAR

Touch	
See	
Hear	
Smell	
Taste	

MONTH	DAY	YEAR

Touch	
See	
Hear	
Smell	
Taste	

MONTH	DAY	YEAR

Touch	
See	
Hear	
Smell	
Taste	

MONTH	DAY	YEAR

Touch	
See	
Hear	
Smell	
Taste	

MONTH	DAY	YEAR

Touch	
See	
Hear	
Smell	
Taste	

MONTH	DAY	YEAR

Touch	
See	
Hear	
Smell	
Taste	

MONTH	DAY	YEAR

Touch	
See	
Hear	
Smell	
Taste	

MONTH	DAY	YEAR

Touch	
See	
Hear	
Smell	
Taste	

MONTH	DAY	YEAR

Touch	
See	
Hear	
Smell	
Taste	

MONTH	DAY	YEAR

Touch	
See	
Hear	
Smell	
Taste	

MONTH	DAY	YEAR

Touch	
See	
Hear	
Smell	
Taste	

MONTH	DAY	YEAR

Touch	
See	
Hear	
Smell	
Taste	

MONTH	DAY	YEAR

Touch	
See	
Hear	
Smell	
Taste	

MONTH	DAY	YEAR

Touch	
See	
Hear	
Smell	
Taste	

Monthly Five-Senses Portrait

Pick a subject for this month's five-senses portrait. You can choose a person, a pet, a place, a trip, a city, yourself, or any other subject you can think of. Identify the sights, sounds, smells, tastes, and touch of all the things and experiences you associate with the subject you chose.

DATE

WHEN I THINK OF...
Write the subject of this month's five-senses portrait.

I THINK OF SEEING...

-
-
-
-
-

I THINK OF HEARING...

-
-
-
-
-

I THINK OF SMELLING...

- ....
- ....
- ....
- ....
- ....

I THINK OF TASTING...

- ....
- ....
- ....
- ....
- ....

I THINK OF TOUCHING...

- ....
- ....
- ....
- ....
- ....

MONTH SIX

This month pay special attention to
how you experience several senses

Together

"The more we know, the more we notice."

–GRETCHEN RUBIN

MONTH	DAY	YEAR

Observation

SENSES USED
Check all that apply.

See · Hear · Smell · Taste · Touch

MONTH	DAY	YEAR

Observation

SENSES USED
Check all that apply.

See · Hear · Smell · Taste · Touch

MONTH	DAY	YEAR

Observation

SENSES USED
Check all that apply.

See Hear Smell Taste Touch

MONTH	DAY	YEAR

Observation

SENSES USED
Check all that apply.

See Hear Smell Taste Touch

MONTH | DAY | YEAR

Observation

SENSES USED
Check all that apply.

See Hear Smell Taste Touch

MONTH | DAY | YEAR

Observation

SENSES USED
Check all that apply.

See Hear Smell Taste Touch

MONTH	DAY	YEAR

Observation

SENSES USED
Check all that apply.

See Hear Smell Taste Touch

MONTH	DAY	YEAR

Observation

SENSES USED
Check all that apply.

See Hear Smell Taste Touch

MONTH	DAY	YEAR

Observation

SENSES USED
Check all that apply.

See Hear Smell Taste Touch

MONTH	DAY	YEAR

Observation

SENSES USED
Check all that apply.

See Hear Smell Taste Touch

MONTH | DAY | YEAR

Observation

SENSES USED
Check all that apply.

See Hear Smell Taste Touch

MONTH | DAY | YEAR

Observation

SENSES USED
Check all that apply.

See Hear Smell Taste Touch

MONTH	DAY	YEAR

Observation

SENSES USED
Check all that apply.

See Hear Smell Taste Touch

MONTH	DAY	YEAR

Observation

SENSES USED
Check all that apply.

See Hear Smell Taste Touch

MONTH | DAY | YEAR

Observation

SENSES USED
Check all that apply.

See Hear Smell Taste Touch

MONTH | DAY | YEAR

Observation

SENSES USED
Check all that apply.

See Hear Smell Taste Touch

MONTH	DAY	YEAR

Observation

SENSES USED
Check all that apply.

See Hear Smell Taste Touch

MONTH	DAY	YEAR

Observation

SENSES USED
Check all that apply.

See Hear Smell Taste Touch

MONTH	DAY	YEAR

Observation

SENSES USED
Check all that apply.

See Hear Smell Taste Touch

MONTH	DAY	YEAR

Observation

SENSES USED
Check all that apply.

See Hear Smell Taste Touch

MONTH	DAY	YEAR

Observation

SENSES USED
Check all that apply.

See Hear Smell Taste Touch

MONTH	DAY	YEAR

Observation

SENSES USED
Check all that apply.

See Hear Smell Taste Touch

MONTH	DAY	YEAR

Observation

SENSES USED
Check all that apply.

See Hear Smell Taste Touch

MONTH	DAY	YEAR

Observation

SENSES USED
Check all that apply.

See Hear Smell Taste Touch

MONTH	DAY	YEAR

Observation

SENSES USED
Check all that apply.

See Hear Smell Taste Touch

MONTH	DAY	YEAR

Observation

SENSES USED
Check all that apply.

See Hear Smell Taste Touch

MONTH | DAY | YEAR

Observation

SENSES USED
Check all that apply.

See Hear Smell Taste Touch

MONTH | DAY | YEAR

Observation

SENSES USED
Check all that apply.

See Hear Smell Taste Touch

MONTH | DAY | YEAR

Observation

SENSES USED
Check all that apply.

See Hear Smell Taste Touch

MONTH | DAY | YEAR

Observation

SENSES USED
Check all that apply.

See Hear Smell Taste Touch

MONTH	DAY	YEAR

Observation

SENSES USED
Check all that apply.

See Hear Smell Taste Touch

Monthly Five-Senses Portrait

Pick a subject for this month's five-senses portrait. You can choose a person, a pet, a place, a trip, a city, yourself, or any other subject you can think of. Identify the sights, sounds, smells, tastes, and touch of all the things and experiences you associate with the subject you chose.

DATE

WHEN I THINK OF...
Write the subject of this month's five-senses portrait.

I THINK OF SEEING...

-
-
-
-
-

I THINK OF HEARING...

-
-
-
-
-

I THINK OF SMELLING...

- ....
- ....
- ....
- ....
- ....

I THINK OF TASTING...

- ....
- ....
- ....
- ....
- ....

I THINK OF TOUCHING...

- ....
- ....
- ....
- ....
- ....

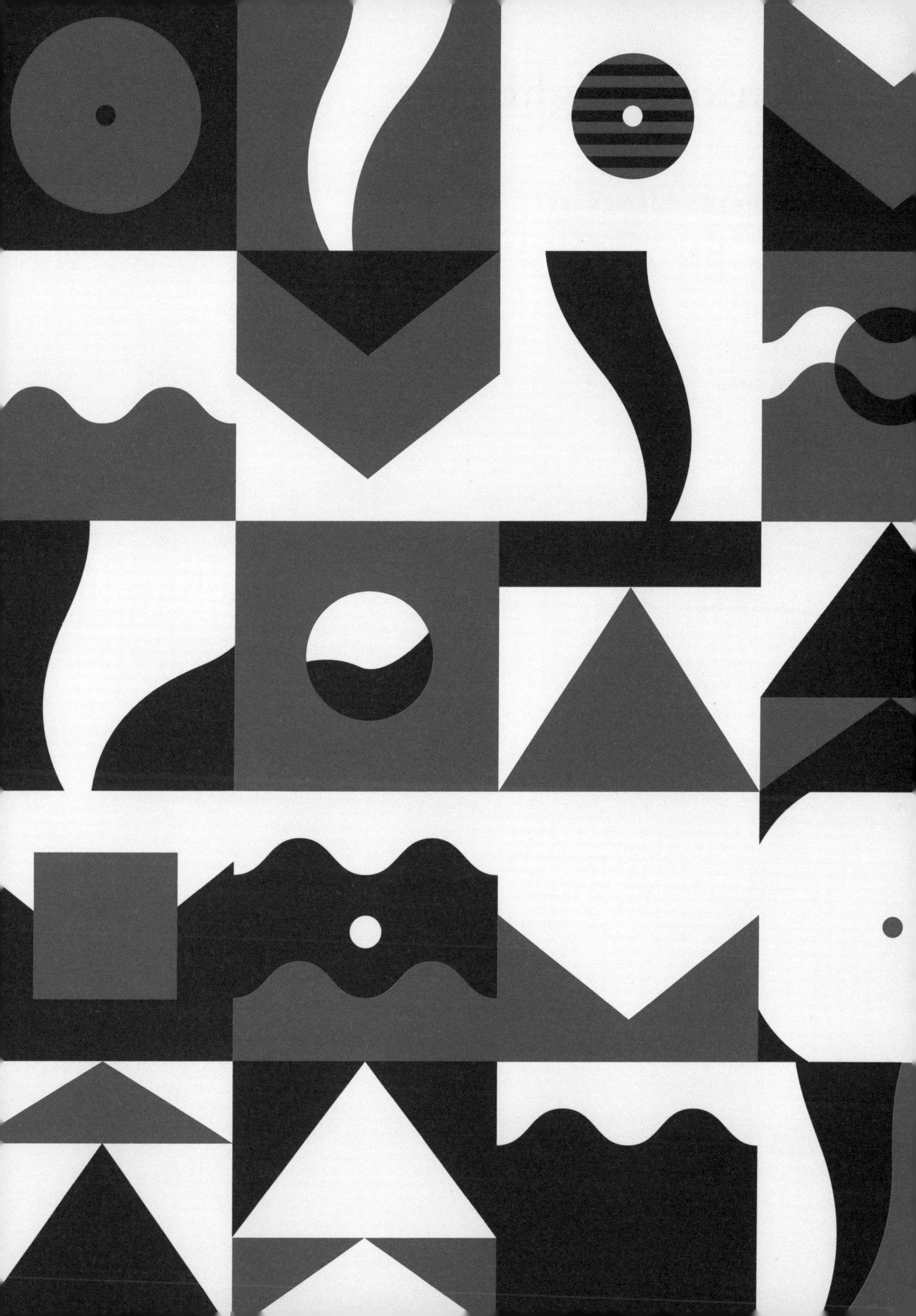

Sensory Highlights

Reflect on the last six months.

EVALUATE YOUR SENSES

On a scale of 1 to 10, rate how aware you are of each of your five senses. 1=need to work more on this sense, 10=mastered this sense entirely.

SEEING

HEARING

SMELLING

TASTING

TOUCHING

REFLECTIONS

Record your thoughts, highlights, and what you've learned.

“SEEING” HIGHLIGHTS OF YOUR SIX MONTHS

Add dates and memories related to your sense of seeing. Fill in as little or as much as you want. See the beginning of the journal for an example.

...... / ...... / ...... →

...... / ...... / ...... →

...... / ...... / ...... →

...... / ...... / ...... →

...... / ...... / ...... →

...... / ...... / ...... →

...... / ...... / ...... →

...... / ...... / ...... →

...... / ...... / ...... →

...... / ...... / ...... →

"HEARING" HIGHLIGHTS OF YOUR SIX MONTHS

Add dates and memories related to your sense of hearing. Fill in as little or as much as you want. See the beginning of the journal for an example.

......./......./....... →

......./......./....... →

......./......./....... →

......./......./....... →

......./......./....... →

......./......./....... →

......./......./....... →

......./......./....... →

......./......./....... →

......./......./....... →

"SMELLING" HIGHLIGHTS OF YOUR SIX MONTHS

Add dates and memories related to your sense of smelling. Fill in as little or as much as you want. See the beginning of the journal for an example.

.... / .... / ....

.... / .... / ....

.... / .... / ....

.... / .... / ....

.... / .... / ....

.... / .... / ....

.... / .... / ....

.... / .... / ....

.... / .... / ....

.... / .... / ....

"TASTING" HIGHLIGHTS OF YOUR SIX MONTHS

Add dates and memories related to your sense of tasting. Fill in as little or as much as you want. See the beginning of the journal for an example.

......../......../........ →

......../......../........ →

......../......../........ →

......../......../........ →

......../......../........ →

......../......../........ →

......../......../........ →

......../......../........ →

......../......../........ →

......../......../........ →

Ⓐ "TOUCHING" HIGHLIGHTS OF YOUR SIX MONTHS

Add dates and memories related to your sense of touching. Fill in as little or as much as you want. See the beginning of the journal for an example.

....../....../......

....../....../......

....../....../......

....../....../......

....../....../......

....../....../......

....../....../......

....../....../......

....../....../......

....../....../......

About Gretchen Rubin

Gretchen Rubin is one of the most thought-provoking and influential writers on the linked subjects of habits, happiness, and human nature. She's the author of many blockbuster *New York Times* bestselling books, including *The Happiness Project* and *Better Than Before*. Her books have sold more than three million copies worldwide, in more than thirty languages. On her award-winning podcast, *Happier with Gretchen Rubin*, she shares insights, strategies, stories, and tips that help people understand themselves and create happier lives. Gretchen started her career in law and was clerking for Supreme Court Justice Sandra Day O'Connor when she realized she wanted to be a writer. She lives in New York City with her husband and two daughters.

To learn more about happiness, habits, and human nature, follow **@gretchenrubin** on social media and sign up for Gretchen's newsletter at **gretchenrubin.com**.

Resources

BOOKS

Gretchen Rubin is the author of many bestselling books on happiness, habits, and human nature. She combines rigorous research with personal observation to help readers know themselves better, and become happier, healthier, more productive, and more creative.

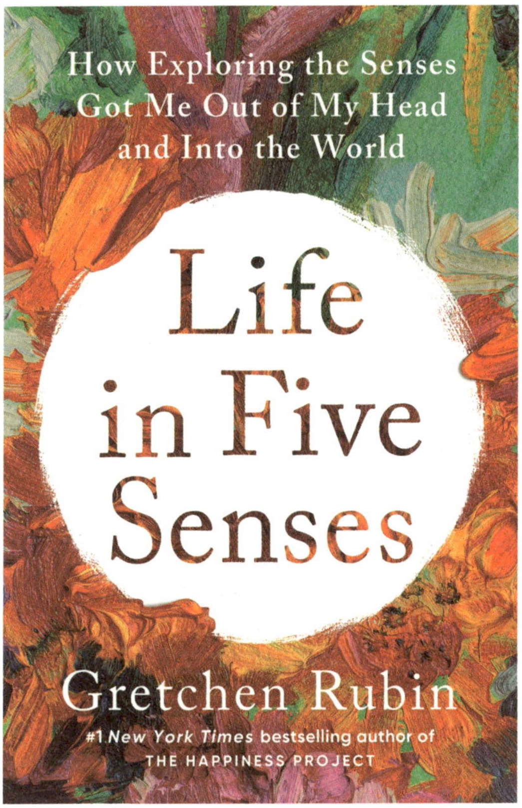

Life in Five Senses

How Exploring The Senses Got Me Out of My Head and Into the World

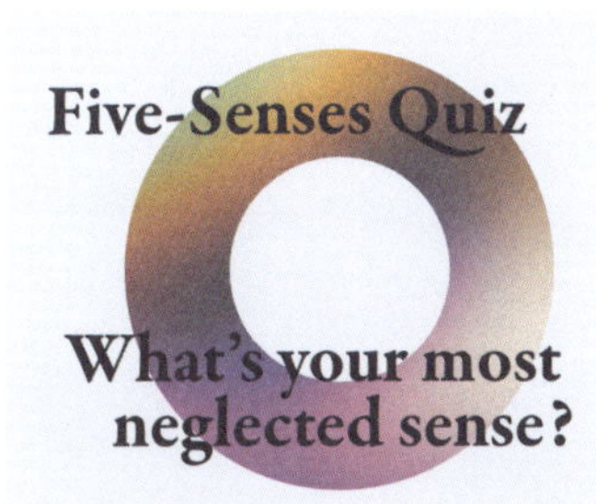

Tapping into a neglected sense can revive our sense of excitement, wonder, and comfort. Take the free **Five-Senses Quiz** to help you identify your most neglected sense, and get tips for deepening your experience.
Visit gretchenrubin.com/quiz.

Better Than Before

What I Learned About Making and Breaking Habits—to Sleep More, Quit Sugar, Procrastinate Less, and Generally Build a Happier Life

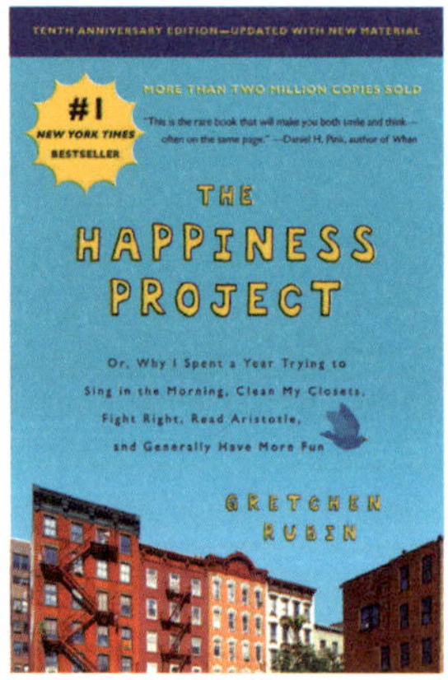

The Happiness Project

Or, Why I Spent a Year Trying to Sing in the Morning, Clean My Closets, Fight Right, Read Aristotle, and Generally Have More Fun

The Four Tendencies

The Indispensable Personality Profiles That Reveal How to Make Your Life Better (and Other People's Lives Better, Too)

Happier at Home

Kiss More, Jump More, Abandon Self-Control, and My Other Experiments in Everyday Life

Outer Order, Inner Calm

Declutter and Organize to Make More Room for Happiness

WEBSITE

Explore Gretchen's articles on popular topics, discover strategies for happiness and habits, take quizzes, and download helpful resources. You can also sign up to receive her free newsletters, which have more than one million subscribers.

Visit gretchenrubin.com.

PODCAST

Every week on *Happier with Gretchen Rubin*, Gretchen brings her practical, manageable insights about happiness and good habits to this lively, thought-provoking podcast. Gretchen's co-host is her younger sister, Elizabeth Craft, a TV writer and producer, who (lovingly) refers to Gretchen as her happiness bully. They explore a wide range of topics, from quick happiness hacks to fascinating discoveries about human nature.

APP

The *Happier*™ app is the practical toolbox to help you start your own Happiness Project and build the habits to create the life you want. Get strategies tailored specifically to you, using Gretchen Rubin's research- and observation-based principles to determine the approach that's most likely to set you up for success.

Download at thehappierapp.com, or from the Apple App Store and Google Play Store.

THE
HAPPINESS
PROJECT

GRETCHEN RUBIN

the-happiness-project.com | gretchenrubin.com

Cover artist: Emmanuelle Joyeux